HE IS RISEN!

Activity Book

He is Risen! Activity Book

Bible Pathway Adventures® is a trademark of BPA Publishing Ltd.
Defenders of the Faith® is a trademark of BPA Publishing Ltd.

ISBN: 978-1-98-858599-4

Author: Pip Reid
Creative Director: Curtis Reid

For free Bible resources including coloring pages, worksheets, puzzles and more, visit our website at:

www.biblepathwayadventures.com

www.biblepathwayadventures.com
He is Risen! Activity Book

2

© BPA Publishing Ltd 2023

◆◇ INTRODUCTION ◇◆

Enjoy teaching your children about the Bible with our *He is Risen! Activity Book*. Packed with detailed lesson plans, coloring pages, fun worksheets, and puzzles to help educators just like you teach children the Biblical faith. Includes scripture references for easy Bible verse look- up and a handy answer key for teachers.

Bible Pathway Adventures helps educators and parents teach children a Biblical faith in a fun and creative way. We do this via our illustrated storybooks, Activity Books, and printable activities – all available on our website: www.biblepathwayadventures.com

Thanks for buying this Activity Book and supporting our ministry. Every book purchased helps us continue our work providing free Classroom Packs and discipleship resources to families and missions around the world.

The search for Truth is more fun than Tradition!

www.biblepathwayadventures.com
He is Risen! Activity Book

3

© BPA Publishing Ltd 2023

◆◇ TABLE OF CONTENTS ◇◆

www.biblepathwayadventures.com
He is Risen! Activity Book

5

© BPA Publishing Ltd 2023

www.biblepathwayadventures.com
He is Risen! Activity Book

6

© BPA Publishing Ltd 202

Our vision is to provide culturally, historically, and biblically sound materials to help you teach your children a Biblical faith. When we read the Bible in the context of the ancient Hebrew culture, it comes alive and unlocks the beauty and richness of the faith.

Why do we use Hebrew names like Yeshua? Or include the Biblical Feasts like the Feast of Unleavened Bread and Pentecost (Shavu'ot)? Because understanding these Hebrew names and festivals helps us unlock the richness of the Biblical account – a richness and understanding that can get lost if we solely view it from a modern Western perspective.

For example, Matthew 26:34 says… "Before the rooster crows, you will deny me three times." In its cultural and historical context, this was not actually a rooster crowing but the Temple Crier, a priest who announced the morning Temple services and sacrifices at the time of Yeshua. Did you know the modern English name of 'Jesus' has only been used for 500 years? This means Mary and the disciples would have called the Messiah by His actual Hebrew name, Yeshua or Yehoshua, which means, 'God saves,' or 'God is my salvation.' Isn't that wonderful!

So…let's take a trip back in time and enjoy the richness of the Bible!

www.biblepathwayadventures.com
He is Risen! Activity Book

7

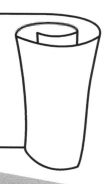

LESSON 1 | Lesson Plan
The last supper

Teacher: _____

Today's Bible passages: Matthew 26:1-56, Luke 22:1-53, John 13:1-18:14

Welcome prayer:
Pray a simple prayer with the children before you begin the lesson.

Lesson objectives:
In this lesson, children will learn:
1. What happened at the 'Last Supper'
2. Which disciple betrayed Yeshua

Did You Know?
In the local Hebrew language, Gethsemane means 'olive press'. Many olive trees grew in the garden of Gethsemane.

Bible lesson overview:
At the start of the Feast of Unleavened Bread, Yeshua (Jesus) and His disciples ate a meal in an upper room in Jerusalem. Yeshua prayed and thanked God for the bread and wine. While they were eating, He said to them, "One of you will betray Me." (After that, Judas went and told the religious leaders where to find Yeshua. He was paid 30 pieces of silver). That evening, our Messiah became like a servant and washed His disciple's feet. He wanted to show them how to serve one another. Then they left the city and walked to a garden on the Mount of Olives. There the religious leaders found Yeshua, arrested Him, and took Him to Annas, the father-in-law Caiaphas, the High Priest. Full of fear, the disciples deserted their Master and ran away.

www.biblepathwayadventures.com
He is Risen! Activity Book

8

© BPA Publishing Ltd 202

Let's Review:

Questions to ask your students:

1. Why did Yeshua and His twelve disciples meet together?
2. How did Judas betray Yeshua?
3. How did Yeshua show His disciples to serve one another?
4. After the meal, where did Yeshua take His disciples?
5. How did the disciples react when Yeshua was arrested?

 A memory verse to help children remember God's Word:

"I am the way, and the truth, and the life. No one comes to the Father except through Me.
(John 14:6)

Activities:

Bible quiz: The last supper
Bible word search: The last supper
Worksheet: Unleavened Bread
Worksheet: Feast of Unleavened Bread
Worksheet: What's the Word?
Bible activity: Pieces of silver
Coloring page: This is My body
Worksheet: The olive tree
Worksheet: What is a disciple?
Complete the picture: Garden of Gethsemane
Bible quiz: Mount of Olives
Worksheet: The religious leaders

Closing prayer:

End the lesson with a prayer.

www.biblepathwayadventures.com
He is Risen! Activity Book

9

© BPA Publishing Ltd 2023

The last SUPPER

Read Matthew 26:1-56, Luke 22:1-53, and John 13:1-18:24. Answer the questions below.

1. Where did Yeshua eat a meal with His disciples before His arrest?

2. What did they eat and drink at the meal?

3. Whose feet did Yeshua wash?

4. Who left the meal to betray Yeshua?

5. What new commandment did Yeshua give His disciples?

6. Who did Yeshua say would deny Him?

7. What dispute arose among the disciples?

8. What will we do if we love the Messiah? (John 14:15)

9. Who did Yeshua say will teach us all things?

10. Where did Yeshua take the disciples after the meal?

www.biblepathwayadventures.com
He is Risen! Activity Book

10

© BPA Publishing Ltd 202

The last SUPPER

Read Matthew 26:1-56, Luke 22:1-53, and John 13:1-18:24.
Find and circle the words below.

```
Z  B  C  T  Q  D  Y  Z  G  D  O  B  U  C  K
L  H  C  I  F  E  O  E  A  W  N  O  X  U  O
Q  J  Y  A  E  A  R  H  S  I  T  D  S  P  R
J  U  D  A  S  W  T  A  A  H  M  Y  Z  O  C
J  K  O  W  S  I  S  H  S  W  U  T  Z  R  O
B  L  O  O  D  L  M  R  E  E  N  A  Y  J  M
K  H  F  Y  S  V  R  S  M  R  O  M  Q  T  M
S  E  M  N  M  Y  L  S  K  I  K  J  E  G  A
Z  C  O  V  E  N  A  N  T  A  N  N  U  K  N
M  W  S  Q  P  G  W  K  N  X  A  F  W  W  D
E  B  D  G  D  Q  H  N  J  L  P  V  P  M
U  P  P  E  R  R  O  O  M  Y  V  O  Z  I  E
B  R  E  A  D  F  M  F  G  W  F  Y  E  N  N
V  G  M  M  D  I  S  C  I  P  L  E  S  P  T
C  G  L  W  A  S  H  F  E  E  T  S  G  K  D
```

COVENANT

BLOOD

BREAD

UPPER ROOM

COMMANDMENT

BODY

JUDAS

FATHER

DISCIPLES

WASH FEET

YESHUA

CUP

www.biblepathwayadventures.com
He is Risen! Activity Book

11

Feast of Unleavened Bread

When the children of Israel left Egypt, they were in such a hurry that they did not have time to let their bread dough rise. So, they carried the unbaked dough on their backs. As they were walking, it cooked in the sun. Because the bread had no yeast, it became hard and flat, and was known as 'matzah'. Eating matzah every year during the Feast of Unleavened Bread reminds people of the Israelites' departure from Egypt and how God delivered them from bondage. Although the Israelites had been freed physically, they still worshipped the false gods of Egypt. They had to learn to leave Egypt spiritually. The Feast of Unleavened Bread begins on the fifteenth day of Nissan (March-April) and lasts for seven days. Many people think the Feast of Unleavened Bread is a Jewish celebration. But the Bible says that this Feast is one of God's 'Appointed Times.'

1. How do you and your family honor the Feast of Unleavened Bread?

....

2. How did God tell the Israelites to prepare their houses for the Feast of Unleavened Bread? (Exodus 12:15-19)

....

Color the matzah!

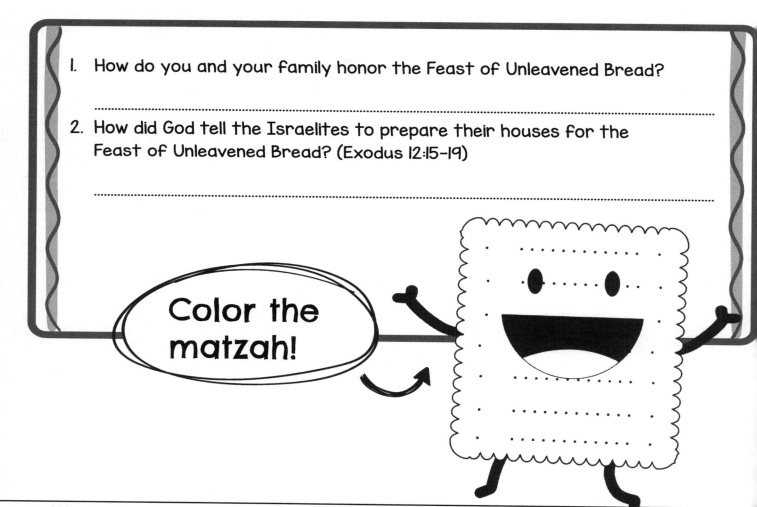

www.biblepathwayadventures.com
He is Risen! Activity Book

12

Unleavened Bread

Draw a picture of a piece of matzah (unleavened bread).

Imagine you are at the Last Supper. What would you say to your Messiah?

....
....
....
....
....
....
....
....

Where in the Bible do I find instructions to honor the Feast of Unleavened Bread?

....
....
....
....
....

If the Last Supper was a book, the cover would look like this...

What's the Word?

Read Matthew 26:20-29 (ESV). Using the words below,
fill in the blanks to complete the Bible passage.

TWELVE	DISH	BETRAY	FORGIVENESS
FRUIT	COVENANT	BREAD	FATHER'S

66 When it was evening, He reclined at table with the .... As they were eating, He said, "Truly I say to you, one of you will betray Me." They were very sorrowful and began to say to Him one after another, "Is it I, Master?" He answered, "He who has dipped his hand in the .... with Me will betray Me. The Son of Man goes as it is written of Him, but woe to that man by whom the Son of Man is betrayed! It would have been better for that man if he had not been born." Judas who would .... Him, answered, "Is it I, Rabbi?" He said to him, "You have said so." Now as they were eating, Yeshua took .... and after blessing it broke it and gave it to the disciples, and said, "Take, eat; this is My body." And He took a cup, and when He had given thanks He gave it to them, saying, "Drink of it, all of you, for this is My blood of the ...., which is poured out for many for the .... of sins. I tell you I will not drink again of this .... of the vine until that day when I drink it new with you in My .... kingdom." 99

www.biblepathwayadventures.com
He is Risen! Activity Book

14

© BPA Publishing Ltd 202

Pieces of silver

Count the number of silver coins in the bag to discover how much money Judas was given to betray Yeshua. What are these silver coins worth today? Color the picture.

" This is my body, which is given for you. Do this in remembrance of Me. "

(Luke 22:19)

www.biblepathwayadventures.com
He is Risen! Activity Book

16

© BPA Publishing Ltd 202

The olive tree

Yeshua spent time with His disciples in the Garden of Gethsemane. The name Gethsemane means 'oil press'. Today, olive presses can still be found throughout the land of Israel. The Hebrews made olive oil by placing olives in sacks and stacking them on top of one another. A beam was lowered onto the stack and weight added to the end of the beam to press oil from the olives. Label the olive tree from the words below. Color the tree.

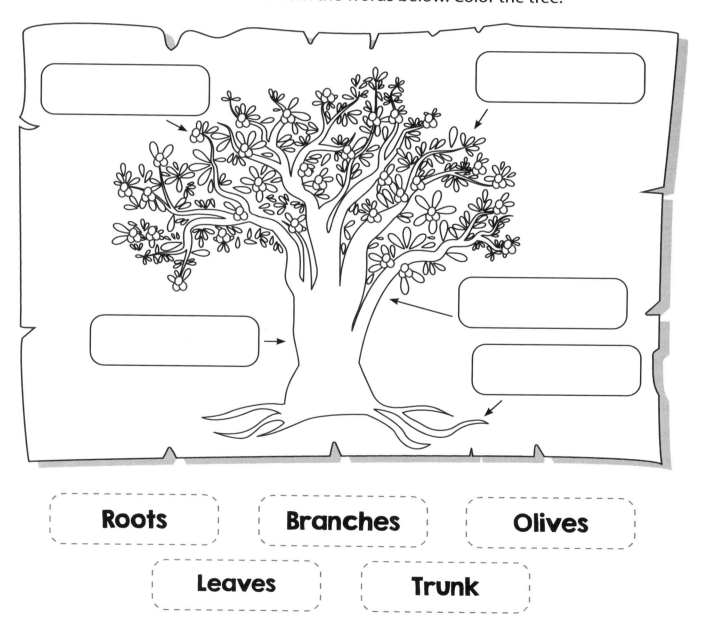

Roots   **Branches**   **Olives**

Leaves   **Trunk**

www.biblepathwayadventures.com
He is Risen! Activity Book

17

© BPA Publishing Ltd 2023

What is a disciple?

Yeshua had twelve disciples. Their names were Simon Peter, Andrew, James (son of Zebedee
John, Philip, Bartholomew, Thomas, Matthew, James (son of Alphaeus), Thaddaeus,
Simon the Zealot and Judas Iscariot. (Matthew 10:1-4 and Luke 6:12-16.)
Let's learn what it means to be a disciple.

Before the time of Yeshua, discipleship was already a well-established process within Hebrew culture.
To become a disciple, you first had to finish Bet Midrash. This was where boys aged 13-15 studied the
entire Tanakh (Old Testament) while learning the family trade. Boys who finished Bet Midrash were then
invited by a teacher to become his disciple. These disciples were known as talmidim and they learned
everything from their teacher. They ate the same food as their teacher ate, they learned to keep the
Sabbath the way their teacher kept the Sabbath, and they studied the Torah exactly the same way as
their teacher. A disciple had four jobs; to memorize his teacher's words, to learn his teacher's traditions
and interpretations, to imitate his teacher, and after he was fully trained, he would become a teacher
and teach disciples of his own.

"Every disciple fully trained will be like his teacher." (Luke 6:40)

I imitate Yeshua everyday by…

....

....

....

....

Color the disciple! ➡

www.biblepathwayadventures.com
He is Risen! Activity Book

18

© BPA Publishing Ltd 202

Garden of Gethsemane

Yeshua prayed in the garden of Gethsemane. While he prayed, three of His disciples (Peter, James, and John) fell asleep. Draw Yeshua and the disciples in the garden.

Mount of OLIVES

Read Matthew 26:1-56, Luke 22:1-53, and John 13:1-18:24.
Answer the questions below.

1. Where did Yeshua eat a meal with His disciples before His arrest?

2. Which garden did Yeshua go to pray in before He was arrested by the religious leaders?

3. While Yeshua was praying, what happened to Peter, James, and John?

4. Which disciple did Yeshua warn would deny Him three times?

5. How did Judas betray Yeshua in the garden?

6. Who appeared to Yeshua in the garden to give Him strength?

7. What did the religious leaders give Judas to betray Yeshua?

8. Which Appointed Time (Feast) had Yeshua come to Jerusalem to keep?

9. What happened to the disciples after Yeshua was arrested?

10. After the temple guards arrested Yeshua, where did they take Him?

www.biblepathwayadventures.com
He is Risen! Activity Book

20

© BPA Publishing Ltd 202

The religious leaders

Judas went to the chief priests and the officers of the temple guard and discussed with them how he might betray Yeshua (Luke 22:4). In first century Judea, the religious leaders at the temple in Jerusalem were important powerful men. Not only did they make the rules about the religious life of the Hebrew people, they were also rulers and judges. The Sanhedrin (Jewish council) was the supreme court of ancient Israel, made up of seventy men and a high priest. At the time of Yeshua and the disciples, the Sanhedrin met in the temple in Jerusalem every day except during the feasts and on the Sabbath.

Many religious leaders (like the chief priests and high priest) lived in luxury. They funded their lavish lifestyles with a temple tax that the Hebrew people had to pay. These temple taxes combined with taxes imposed by Herod and Rome were a huge burden that kept many people in poverty. No wonder the Hebrews eagerly waited for a Savior to overthrow the Roman rulers and take back the scepter to become the true ruling king of Israel.

1. Why were the religious leaders so powerful?

    ....

2. Why do you think the Hebrew people were eagerly awaiting a Savior?

    ....

Color the
religious leader!

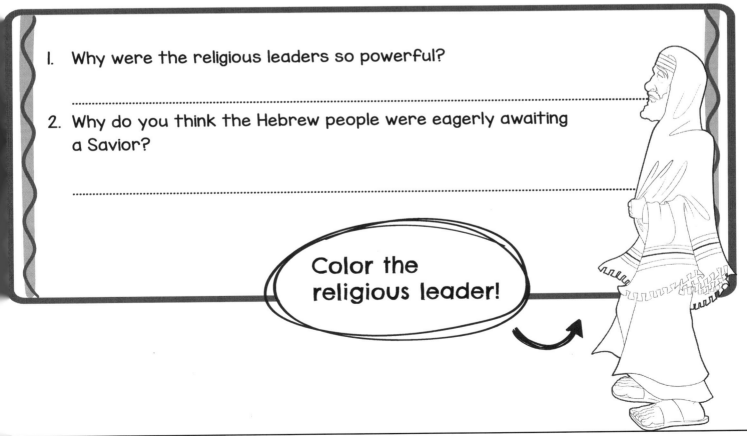

www.biblepathwayadventures.com
He is Risen! Activity Book

21

LESSON 2 | **Lesson Plan**
Road to Golgotha

Teacher: _____

Today's Bible passages: Matthew 26:57-27:2, Mark 15:1-32

Welcome prayer:
Pray a simple prayer with the children before you begin the lesson.

Lesson objectives:
In this lesson, children will learn:
1. How the religious leaders had Yeshua sentenced to death
2. Why Judas returned 30 pieces of silver

Did You Know?
Crucifixion was a common form of execution throughout the Roman Empire. The Romans lined roads into cities with bodies hung on crosses to install fear in the people.

Bible lesson overview:
Caiaphas (the High Priest) and the Sanhedrin (Jewish Council) wanted to get rid of Yeshua. After a mock trial, they took Him to Pilate, the Roman governor. Only Pilate could have Yeshua put to death. Pilate listened to the religious leaders and sentenced Yeshua to die by crucifixion. When Judas saw they had decided to kill Yeshua, he changed his mind and returned the money he was paid to betray Him. But it was too late. Roman soldiers forced Yeshua to carry a crossbeam through the streets of Jerusalem to a place called Golgotha. There, Roman soldiers nailed Him to a stake (which formed a cross). Above His head they put a sign that said, 'This is the king of the Jews'. Beside Him they placed two criminals.

www.biblepathwayadventures.com
He is Risen! Activity Book

22

© BPA Publishing Ltd 202

Let's Review:

Questions to ask your students:

1. Who was the Sanhedrin?
2. Why did the religious leaders ask Pilate to put Yeshua to death?
3. Why did Judas return the money?
4. Where was Yeshua nailed to a stake?
5. Who was crucified beside Yeshua at Golgotha?

 A memory verse to help children remember God's Word:

"The soldiers nailed Yeshua to a cross." (Mark 15:24)

Activities:

Worksheet: Who were the Zealots?
Worksheet: Did You Know?
Bible quiz: Pontius Pilate
Coloring page: Journey to Golgotha
Worksheet: Who was Pontius Pilate?
Bible activity: Label a roman soldier
Worksheet: The Temple Crier
Question 'n color: Journey to Golgotha
Recipe: Bake a crown of thorns
Bible quiz: Betrayal
Worksheet: The Jerusalem Times
Worksheet: Golgotha

 Closing prayer:

End the lesson with a prayer.

www.biblepathwayadventures.com
He is Risen! Activity Book

23

© BPA Publishing Ltd 2023

Who were the Zealots?

Why did Peter deny and Judas betray Yeshua? Some historians argue that both men were Zealots, members of a first-century political movement among the Jews who wanted to overthrow the occupying Roman government. They believed that if the people of Israel turned back to God and started war against the Romans, the Messiah would rise up and establish His Kingdom. They did not believe that the Savior would be divine; they were looking for a Savior like King David who would lead a revolution.

According to the Jewish historian Josephus, "the Zealots agree in all other things with the Pharisaic notions; but they have an inviolable attachment to liberty, and say that God is to be their only Ruler and Lord." (Antiquities 18.1.6)

Initially, Yeshua's teachings may have interested the Zealots. They appeared to fit their idea of a Messiah who would turn the Hebrew people back to God. His miracles and healings only added to this perception. But as Yeshua began teaching His disciples that He would die, zealots like Peter and Judas became concerned Yeshua's references to the kingdom were different to their own ideas.

What do you think? Were Peter and Judas zealots? Why / why not?

....

....

....

....

www.biblepathwayadventures.com
He is Risen! Activity Book

24

Did you know?

Some bible scholars believe Judas betrayed Yeshua because he was disappointed Yeshua had not overthrown the Roman rulers. Judas believed that by arranging Yeshua's arrest, he could force Yeshua to reveal Himself as the next king of Israel. He did not understand the Scriptures that showed Yeshua would come as a suffering servant (Isaiah 53). When Yeshua comes again, He will come as the Lion of the tribe of Judah (Revelation 5:5).

"Behold, the Lion of the tribe of Judah, the Root of David, has conquered..." (Revelation 5:5).

Use this space to draw the Lion of the tribe of Judah

Pontius PILATE

Read Matthew 27:1-88 and John 18. Answer the questions below.

1. What was Pilate's job?

2. In which city was Pilate's headquarters?

3. On what seat did Pilate sit to meet Yeshua?

4. Which prisoner did Pilate release?

5. What did Pilate's wife say in a message to Pilate?

6. What did the crowd tell Pilate to do with Yeshua?

7. What did Pilate say to the crowd while he washed his hands?

8. What type of crown did the soldiers put on Yeshua's head?

9. Who went to Pilate and asked for Yeshua's body?

10. Why did Pilate send Roman soldiers to seal the tomb?

www.biblepathwayadventures.com
He is Risen! Activity Book

26

© BPA Publishing Ltd 202

"And they led Him out to crucify Him..."

(Mark 15:20)

www.biblepathwayadventures.com

le is Risen! Activity Book

© BPA Publishing Ltd 2023

Who was Pontius Pilate?

This article introduces Pontius Pilate. As you read it, think about the type of man who sentenced Yeshua to die. Answer the questions below.

Pontius Pilate

At the time of Yeshua's death, Pontius Pilate was the Roman governor of Judea and Samaria. His job was to collect taxes, build roads, and govern this region of the Roman Empire. Pilate was not a popular governor. In a letter from Agrippa I, Pilate was accused of harsh behavior, pride, violence, greed, holding executions without trial, and horrible cruelty. In 36 AD, three years after he sentenced Yeshua to death, Pilate was called back to Rome for questioning about harsh management of an incident involving the Jewish people. Some historians claim that Pilate later committed suicide. Others say Emperor Nero executed him. Another tradition says that He finally accepted Yeshua and was executed by Emperor Tiberius.

In 1961, archaeologists found a limestone block in an ancient Roman amphitheater near Caesarea-on-the-Sea (Maritima). On its face is an inscription, part of a larger dedication to Tiberius Caesar, which says that it was from "Pontius Pilate, Prefect of Judea." Visitors to Caesarea today see a replica limestone block since the original is in the Israel Museum in Jerusalem.

Questions:

Why was Pilate not a popular governor?

....

What did archaeologists find that proves Pilate once governed Judea?

....

Label a Roman soldier

At the time of Yeshua and the disciples, the Roman Empire ruled Judea. Roman soldiers wore and carried heavy armor. Using the Internet or an encyclopedia, research the type of clothing worn by Roman soldiers. Label the pieces of armor on the soldier. Color the picture.

(a) helmet

(b) woolen tunic

(c) arm protection

(d) sandals

(e) body armor

(f) shoulder plate

(g) cloak

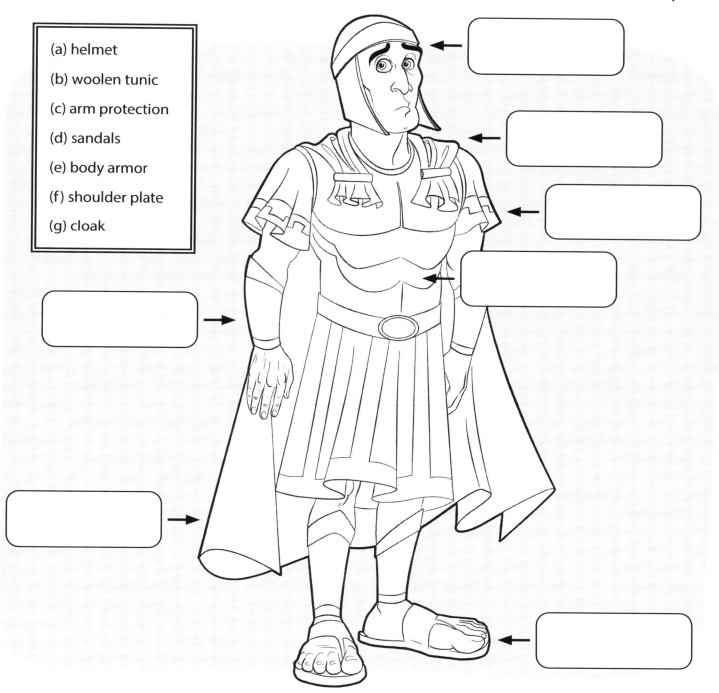

The Temple Crier

What sound did Peter hear in the courtyard of the High Priest's palace? Was it the Temple Crier, or a rooster crowing? Given chickens were forbidden in Jerusalem during temple times, (Josephus the historian and others confirm this by stating that chickens were banned as they flew into and defiled the temple), perhaps the 'rooster' or 'cock' that Peter heard was actually a man?

That man was a priest at the temple. He was responsible for unlocking the temple doors every morning and calling all the priests, Levites, and Israelites to begin preparing for the morning sacrifice service. He would cry out three statements in a loud voice: "All the priests prepare to sacrifice. All the Levites to their stations. All the Israelites come to worship." This priest was known as the Temple Crier, and was called 'alektor' in Greek, which can be translated as a 'cock' or 'man'. Was 'alektor' assumed to be a 'cock' or 'rooster' instead of the priestly Temple Crier?

1. Why were chickens forbidden in Jerusalem during temple times?

   ----

2. What do you think? Did Peter hear the Temple Crier or a rooster crow?

Color the Temple Crier!

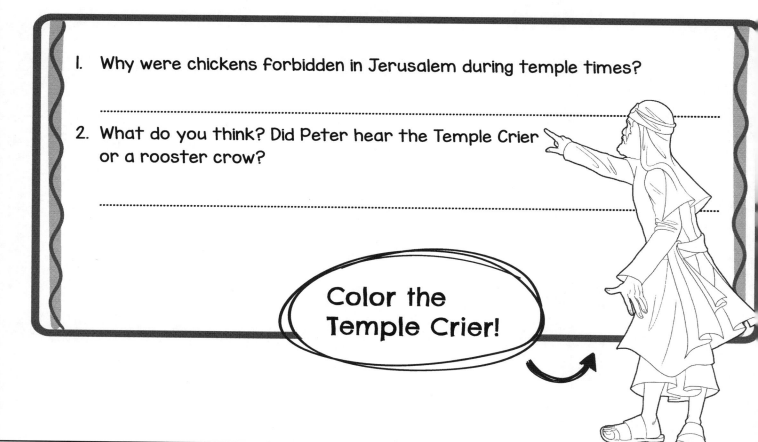

www.biblepathwayadventures.com
He is Risen! Activity Book

30

Journey to Golgotha

Open your Bibles and read John 19.
Answer the questions. Color the picture.

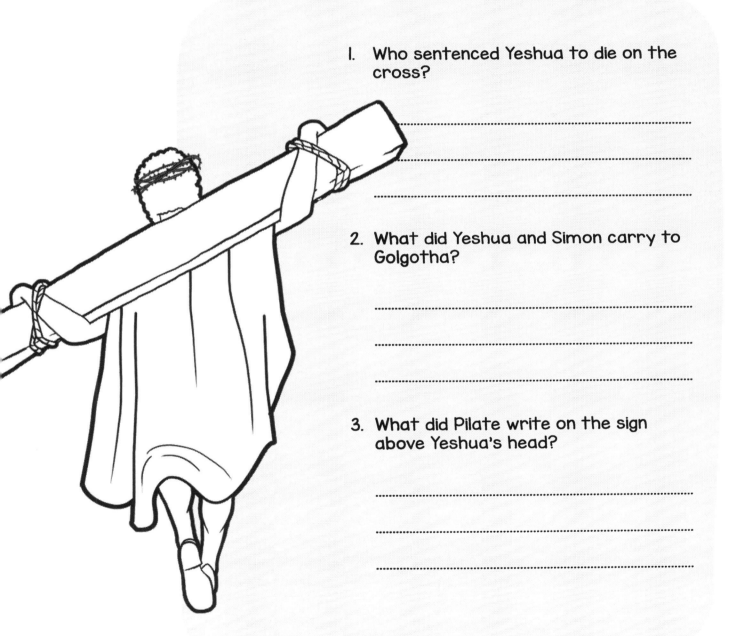

1. Who sentenced Yeshua to die on the cross?

   _____

   _____

   _____

2. What did Yeshua and Simon carry to Golgotha?

   _____

   _____

   _____

3. What did Pilate write on the sign above Yeshua's head?

   _____

   _____

   _____

www.biblepathwayadventures.com
le is Risen! Activity Book

31

Bake a crown of thorns

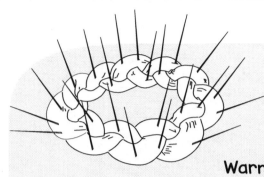

INGREDIENTS

4 cups of flour
1 cup of salt
Warm water to moisten the dough
Wooden toothpicks

METHOD

Preheat your oven to 350° F.
Combine the flour and salt in a large bowl.
Add enough water to make the dough sticky.
Mold the clay into three strands of dough. Braid the dough and form a circle.
Bake in the oven at 350° F for 30 minutes, or until hard and dry.
Remove from oven. When cool, place wooden toothpicks (thorns) in crown.

www.biblepathwayadventures.com
He is Risen! Activity Book

32

BETRAYAL

Read Matthew 26-27, Mark 14, Luke 6, 22, and John 12-13, 18, 21. Answer the questions below.

1. Judas was one of Yeshua's _____.

2. At their last meal together, what did Yeshua give Judas as a sign that he would betray Him?

3. Who paid Judas to betray Yeshua?

4. How much money was Judas paid to betray Yeshua?

5. In which garden did Judas betray Yeshua?

6. How did Judas betray Yeshua?

7. How did Judas address Yeshua in the garden?

8. What was the name of the field purchased with the money Judas returned?

9. After Yeshua rose to heaven, who were the two men put forward to replace Judas?

10. Which man was chosen to replace Judas?

www.biblepathwayadventures.com
le is Risen! Activity Book

33

© BPA Publishing Ltd 2023

City of Jerusalem

The
Jerusalem Times

LAND OF ISRAEL   A PASSOVER PUBLICATION

Barabbas freed!

Caiaphas condemns Messiah

....

....

....

....

....

....

....

....

....

....

City lamb shortage

www.biblepathwayadventures.com
He is Risen! Activity Book

34

© BPA Publishing Ltd 202

Golgotha

Draw a picture of the crucifixion scene at Golgotha.

Imagine you are Judas. What would you say to the religious leaders when you returned the money?

....

....

....

....

....

....

....

Finish this sentence:
Yeshua died so…

....

....

....

....

....

Draw a Roman soldier at Golgotha.

www.biblepathwayadventures.com
e is Risen! Activity Book

35

LESSON 3 | Lesson Plan
The crucifixion

Teacher: _____

Today's Bible passage: Mark 15:16-41

Welcome prayer:
Pray a simple prayer with the children before you begin the lesson.

Lesson objectives:
In this lesson, children will learn:
1. What happened in Jerusalem the day Yeshua was crucified
2. What happened at the temple while Yeshua hung on the cross

Did You Know?
Yeshua died on the cross at the same time the Passover lambs were being killed at the temple in Jerusalem.

Bible lesson overview:
While Yeshua hung on a cross at Golgotha between two criminals, people stopped and mocked Him, including many religious leaders. At midday a strange darkness fell over Jerusalem and the sun stopped shining for three hours. During this time, thousands of Passover lambs were killed at the temple for the Passover meal. Later that afternoon, Yeshua gave up His spirit and died. Strange things began to happen around Jerusalem. An earthquake shook the city and a veil at the temple ripped from top to bottom. At Golgotha, a Roman soldier pierced Yeshua's side with a spear. Blood and water poured out of His body, onto the earth.

www.biblepathwayadventures.com
He is Risen! Activity Book

36

© BPA Publishing Ltd 202

Let's Review:

Questions to ask your students:

1. What did people say to Yeshua while He hung on the cross?
2. What happened at the temple while Yeshua hung on the cross?
3. What were Yeshua's last words before He died?
4. Name three things that happened after Yeshua died?
5. How did the Roman soldier pierce Yeshua's side?

A memory verse to help children remember God's Word:

"Greater love has no one than this, that one lay down his life for his friends." (John 15:13)

Activities:

Bible quiz: Death on the stake
Coloring worksheet: Crucifixion
Coloring page: The Passover
Bible quiz: The Passover meal
Bible craft: Make a paper plate Golgotha
Worksheet: The Passover meal
Bible word scramble: Who pierced the Messiah's body?
Worksheet: The crucifixion
Bible crossword: The cross and empty tomb
Worksheet: The temple
Worksheet: True or false?
Let's learn Hebrew: Passover

Closing prayer:

End the lesson with a prayer.

www.biblepathwayadventures.com
He is Risen! Activity Book

37

Death on the STAKE

Read Matthew 27:32-56. Answer the questions below.

1. Who sentenced Yeshua to die?

2. Who was forced to carry Yeshua's crossbeam through the streets of Jerusalem?

3. At which place outside Jerusalem was Yeshua nailed to the stake?

4. What was written on the sign above Yeshua's head?

5. What did Yeshua cry out while he was nailed to the stake?

6. Who was crucified next to Yeshua?

7. After Yeshua died, how long did darkness cover the land?

8. Who asked Pilate for Yeshua's body?

9. What did the Roman soldier use to pierce Yeshua's side?

10. What was Yeshua wrapped in before he was buried?

Crucifixion

Read Matthew 27:50-52 and write the Bible verses below.

....

....

....

1. What tore into two pieces when Yeshua gave up His spirit?

....

....

2. What shook the city after Yeshua died?

....

....

3. Who said, "Surely He was the Son of God!"?

....

....

Draw your favorite scene from this story.

What could the life of Yeshua teach me?	God used Yeshua to…
....	....

"... take some blood and put it on the two doorposts and lintel of the houses..."

(Exodus 12:7)

www.biblepathwayadventures.com
He is Risen! Activity Book

40

© BPA Publishing Ltd 202

The Passover MEAL

Read Exodus 12:1-32 and Matthew 1, 27.
Answer the questions below.

1. How many plagues did God send on Egypt?

2. How did the Hebrews protect themselves from the final plague?

3. On which day did God tell the Hebrews to find a Passover lamb?

4. On which day were the Hebrews told to kill their Passover lamb?

5. What food did the Israelites eat for the first Passover meal?

6. What type of bread did the Israelites take with them when they left Egypt?

7. The Passover takes place at the start of which Appointed Time?

8. For how long were the Israelites told to observe this meal?

9. In which place outside Jerusalem was Yeshua crucified?

10. Yeshua was of which tribe of Israel?

The Passover Meal

What do you eat for the Passover meal? Draw the food
you eat on the plate below.

www.biblepathwayadventures.com
He is Risen! Activity Book

42

Who pierced the Messiah's body?

Unscramble the words to find the answer. *Hint: Read John 19:34 (ESV).*

"Btu noe fo hte lrsoesdi

_____

rpdicee sih sied ithw a apesr,

_____

and ta eocn reteh meca tuo

_____

bdolo dna tewra."

_____

The crucifixion

Read Exodus 12, Matthew 26, and John 18. Discuss how the pictures below relate to the story of the crucifixion. Match each word with the correct picture.

temple

lamb

Pilate

passover

crown

www.biblepathwayadventures.com
He is Risen! Activity Book

44

© BPA Publishing Ltd 202

The cross and EMPTY TOMB

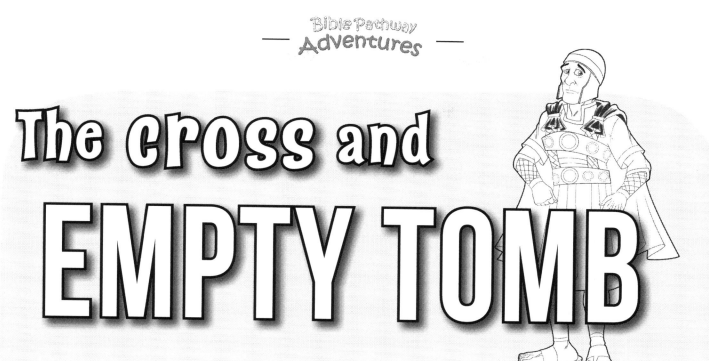

Read Matthew 28, Mark 16, Luke 24, John 20, and Acts 1 (ESV).
Complete the crossword below.

ACROSS

3) Name of the place where Yeshua was crucified.

6) The Roman governor who sentenced Yeshua to die.

7) This type of spiritual being opened the tomb.

8) Yeshua was crucified on this Roman device.

9) Yeshua rose from the grave on which Feast (Appointed Time)?

DOWN

1) After Yeshua died, this shook the city.

2) Yeshua met his disciples by this sea.

4) The disciple who betrayed Yeshua.

5) What was torn from top to bottom inside the temple?

6) This disciple jumped out of the boat and swam to Yeshua.

www.biblepathwayadventures.com
He is Risen! Activity Book

45

© BPA Publishing Ltd 2023

The temple

During Bible times, the temple in Jerusalem was the center of Hebrew life. It began with the construction of the first temple by King Solomon, and ended with its destruction by the Romans in 70 AD. To house the Ark of the Covenant, King Solomon built the first temple in the 10th century BC, which was later destroyed by the Babylonians. They stole all its precious items and burned what remained. A second temple was constructed during the time of Nehemiah and underwent major renovation during the reign of King Herod.

One reason King Herod enlarged the Temple Mount was to accommodate the large number of pilgrims who came to Jerusalem to honor the Passover and Feast of Unleavened Bread, Pentecost (Shavu'ot), and Tabernacles (Sukkot). During the Passover sacrifice at the temple, those who wished to sacrifice formed groups. The Passover lamb, unlike the usual animal offerings, was sacrificed by the Israelites themselves. As with all peace offerings, it was offered in the inner court and its blood tossed on the altar. After one group completed the ritual, the doors were opened again and the next group entered. The lambs were roasted and eaten that night.

I. Why did Herod renovate the temple in Jerusalem?

....

2 How did the Israelites sacrifice their Passover lambs?

....

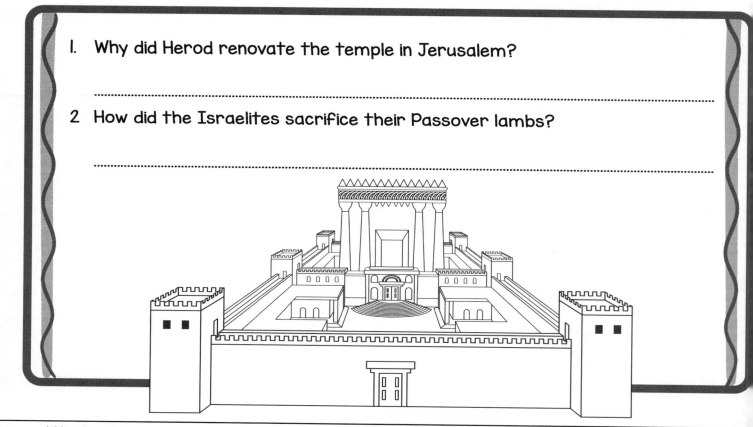

www.biblepathwayadventures.com
He is Risen! Activity Book

46

© BPA Publishing Ltd 202

True or False?

Are the statements below TRUE or FALSE?
Read John 19, Matthew 27, and Luke 23. Circle the correct box below.

The soldiers divided Yeshua's garments into six parts.	TRUE / FALSE
The soldiers broke Yeshua's legs.	TRUE / FALSE
Blood and water poured out of Yeshua's body.	TRUE / FALSE
After Yeshua died, many holy people who had died were raised to life.	TRUE / FALSE
There was a notice above Yeshua's head, which read: This is the king of the Jews.	TRUE / FALSE
Yeshua saw His grandfather standing near the cross.	TRUE / FALSE

Are these statements true or false?

Pesach

The Hebrew name for Passover is Pesach. Before the congregation of Israel left the land of Egypt, they ate a meal of lamb, unleavened bread, and bitter herbs. God asked the Israelites to honor this Appointed Time forever (Exodus 12:14).

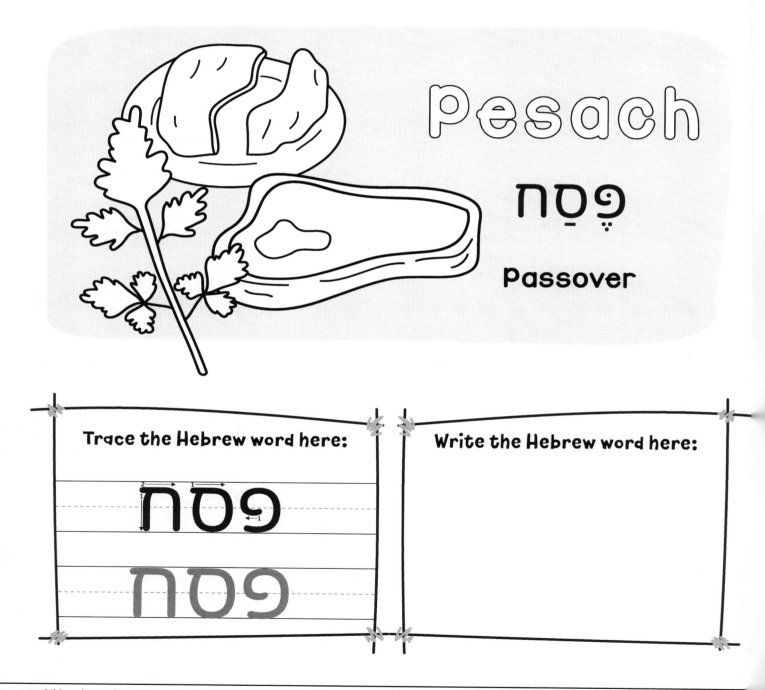

Pesach

פֶּסַח

Passover

Trace the Hebrew word here:

פסח

פסח

Write the Hebrew word here:

www.biblepathwayadventures.com
He is Risen! Activity Book

48

© BPA Publishing Ltd 202

Let's write!

Practice writing 'Pesach' on the lines below.

פסח

פסח

Try this on your own.
Remember that Hebrew is read from RIGHT to LEFT.

www.biblepathwayadventures.com
le is Risen! Activity Book

49

© BPA Publishing Ltd 2023

LESSON 4 | Lesson Plan
He is Risen!

Teacher: _____

Today's Bible passage: Matthew 27:57-28:15

Welcome prayer:
Pray a simple prayer with the children before you begin the lesson.

Lesson objectives:
In this lesson, children will learn:
1. What happened to Yeshua after He died on the cross
2. When Yeshua rose from the grave

Did You Know?
In the land of Israel, rich men were buried in their own tombs made out of solid rock.

Bible lesson overview:
That evening, a secret disciple of Yeshua named Joseph asked Pilate for Yeshua's body. Pilate ordered it be given to him. Joseph took the body, wrapped it in clean linen cloth, and laid it inside his own rock tomb. The priests were worried - Yeshua's disciples might steal Him out of the tomb. Pilate agreed to seal it shut. But God's plans always prevail. On the Feast of First Fruits, Yeshua was resurrected from the dead. Terrified guards raced into the city and told the priests that Yeshua's body was gone! Afraid that people would discover what had happened, they paid the guards a bribe to lie about His disappearance. "Tell people, 'His disciples stole Him away while we were asleep.'" And the guards did so.

www.biblepathwayadventures.com
He is Risen! Activity Book

50

© BPA Publishing Ltd 202

Let's Review:

Questions to ask your students:

1. Who asked Pilate for Yeshua's body?
2. Why did the religious leaders want to seal the tomb shut?
3. Who opened the tomb?
4. What did the angel tell Mary Magdalene and the other Mary outside the tomb?
5. What did the religious leaders do when they heard that Yeshua was missing?

 A memory verse to help children remember God's Word:

"He is risen! He is not here. See the place where they laid Him." (Mark 16:6)

Activities:

Coloring page: He is Risen!
Bible quiz: The resurrection
Bible word search: He is risen!
Worksheet: The chief priests
Worksheet: What is a bribe?
Worksheet: What's the Word?
Worksheet: The Jerusalem Times
Worksheet: Resurrection!
Bible quiz: Mary Magdalene
Coloring worksheet: Mary Magdalene
Fact sheet: Feast of first fruits
Bible verse copywork: Feast of First Fruits
Bible craft: Make a paper plate tomb

 Closing prayer:

End the lesson with a prayer.

www.biblepathwayadventures.com
He is Risen! Activity Book

51

He is Risen!

Yeshua rose from the grave on the Feast of First Fruits. Beside the tomb, draw the angel and two Roman soldiers. Color the picture.

www.biblepathwayadventures.com
He is Risen! Activity Book

52

© BPA Publishing Ltd 202

The
RESURRECTION

Read Matthew 28, Mark 16, Luke 24, John 20, and Acts 1.
Answer the questions below.

① Who rolled away Yeshua's tomb stone?

② During which Appointed Time was Yeshua raised from the grave?

③ What did the priests give the Roman guards to keep quiet?

④ Which woman met Yeshua outside the tomb?

⑤ When Mary Magdalene, Mary mother of James, and Salome went to the tomb with their spices, what did they find?

⑥ What did the two strangers say to the women outside the tomb?

⑦ Which disciple doubted Yeshua was alive?

⑧ While the disciples waited for Yeshua, where did they go fishing?

⑨ How long did Yeshua stay on earth after His resurrection before He rose to Heaven?

⑩ What were Yeshua's final instructions to His disciples?

www.biblepathwayadventures.com
He is Risen! Activity Book

53

He is RISEN!

Read Matthew 28, Mark 16, Luke 24, John 20, and Acts 1.
Find and circle the words below.

```
S E G U A R D S Y M M K F N X
F T A X I B I U Q J E K B X N
I I O R Z G R X R H S F B Y C
P C R N T G E W H R S Y R G L
S O P S E H H V N J I J I A P
Y N C I T G Q H F E A E S R V
R C N R Y F M U M C H R E D U
Y Y J S K G R K A D Z U N E A
F E J U E W V U R K W S G N N
T Z S R Y S K G I O E A Z D G
Q A S H B W S Z B T B L Y Q E
U S U B U A B W J F S E F A L
J M E S H A O X F D I M Y R K
A P P O I N T E D T I M E S X
D I S C I P L E S Z V Z T Q S
```

RISEN

GUARDS

MESSIAH

FIRST FRUITS

STONE

GARDEN

JERUSALEM

DISCIPLES

EARTHQUAKE

ANGEL

YESHUA

APPOINTED TIME

www.biblepathwayadventures.com
He is Risen! Activity Book

54

© BPA Publishing Ltd 202

THE CHIEF PRIESTS

Why do you think the priests told the soldiers to keep quiet?

Read Matthew 28. Who told the chief priests that Yeshua was gone?

....

....

....

....

....

What did the chief priests give the soldiers to keep quiet?

....

....

What did the chief priests tell the soldiers to say about Yeshua's disappearance?

....

....

What is a bribe?

"And you shall take no bribe, for a bribe blinds the clear-sighted and subverts the cause of those who are in the right." (Exodus 23:8)

A group of religious leaders gave the Roman soldiers money to keep quiet about Yeshua's resurrection. The money offered to them was a bribe. What does it mean to bribe someone? Bribery means offering something (e.g. money) to a person in return for a favor. Bribery can be a crime. For example, if a person wanted to take an item into a country that was forbidden or taxable, they could offer the customs officer a bribe to persuade him/her to let them through. In certain countries, some corrupt people will not do their jobs unless they receive a bribe on top of their normal pay. People who are found to be taking bribes can sometimes lose their jobs. The Bible condemns this practice and instead encourages people to practice integrity and honesty (Exodus 23:8, Proverbs 17:23, and Deuteronomy 16:19).

It is wrong to bribe someone because...

....

....

....

....

Color the bribe-taker ➡

Some information on this page cited from *Bribery Facts for Kids. Kiddle Encyclopedia.*

www.biblepathwayadventures.com
He is Risen! Activity Book

56

What's the Word?

Read Matthew 28:1-7 (ESV). Using the words below,
fill in the blanks to complete the Bible passage.

SABBATH	HEAVEN	ANGEL	GALILEE	TREMBLED
MAGDALENE	LIGHTNING	YESHUA	TOMB	DISCIPLES

" After the .... toward the dawn of the first day of the week, Mary .... and the other Mary went to see the .... And behold, there was a great earthquake, for an angel of God descended from .... and rolled back the stone and sat on it. His appearance was like .... and his clothing white as snow. And for fear of him the guards .... and became like dead men. But the .... said to the women, "Do not be afraid, for I know that you seek .... who was crucified. He is not here, for He has risen, as he said. Come, see the place where He lay. Then go quickly and tell His .... that He has risen from the dead. He is going before you to ....; there you will see Him." "

City of Jerusalem

The
Jerusalem Times

FEAST OF FIRST FRUITS

A BIBLE HISTORY PUBLICATION

Missing Messiah!

....

....

....

....

....

....

Angel seen at tomb

....

....

....

....

Barley harvest starts

www.biblepathwayadventures.com
He is Risen! Activity Book

58

© BPA Publishing Ltd 202

Resurrection!

Draw a picture of an angel opening the tomb.

Imagine you are guarding Yeshua's tomb. What would you say to the other guard when you saw the angel of God?

....

....

....

....

....

....

....

The story of the resurrection teaches me…

....

....

....

....

....

If the resurrection was a book, the cover would look like this…

www.biblepathwayadventures.com
He is Risen! Activity Book

59

Mary MAGDALENE

Read Matthew 27-28, Luke 8, 24, Mark 15-16, and John 19-20.
Answer the questions below.

1. How many demons did Yeshua cast out of Mary Magdalene?

2. Who stood at the foot of the cross with Mary Magdalene?

3. Who did Mary see wrapping Yeshua's body in linen cloth?

4. After what day did Mary Magdalene, Mary and Salome buy burial spices?

5. What did they discuss on the way to the tomb?

6. Who told Mary Magdalene that Yeshua had risen?

7. Who did Yeshua first appear to after His resurrection?

8. When Yeshua spoke to Mary at the tomb, who did she think He was?

9. Why did Yeshua tell Mary Magdalene not to touch Him?

10. After Mary saw Yeshua, what did she tell the disciples?

www.biblepathwayadventures.com
He is Risen! Activity Book

60

© BPA Publishing Ltd 202

Mary Magdalene

Read John 20:18 and write the Bible verse below.

....

....

....

1. Who told Mary that Yeshua had risen?

....

....

2. Who did Yeshua first appear to after His resurrection?

....

....

3. What did Mary tell the disciples after she had seen Yeshua?

....

....

Draw your favorite scene from this story.

What could the life of Mary Magdalene teach me?	God used Mary Magdalene to...
....	....
....	....

Feast of First Fruits

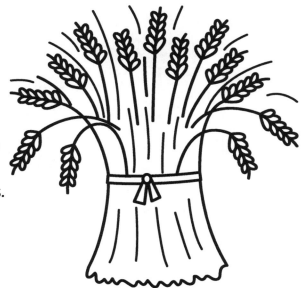

The Feast of Unleavened Bread was a busy time in Jerusalem. Between 250,000 to 500,000 pilgrims came to keep this Appointed Time. Some slept in Jerusalem, while others stayed in nearby villages or in tents around the city. Pilgrims visited the temple, listened to teachers, and bought gifts to take home. There was a great deal of activity, festivity, and many opportunities to make new friends and renew old friendships.

During this time, the Feast of First Fruits (Yom HaBikkurim) took place. It fell on the day after the Sabbath during the Feast of Unleavened Bread. The Feast of First Fruits is one of God's Appointed Times, and in biblical times, it was the job of the high priest to wave the first sheaf (usually a barley cluster known as the first of the first fruits) before God at the temple, with accompanying sacrifices. Only after this ceremony could Israelites harvest the fruit and grain they had grown. The Feast of First Fruits points to Yeshua's resurrection as the first fruits of the righteous. He was resurrected on this very day, which is a reason the apostle Paul said, "But in fact Yeshua has been raised from the dead, the firstfruits of those who have fallen asleep." (1 Corinthians 15:20)

How did the ancient Israelites honor the Feast of First Fruits?

....

How do you honor the Feast of First Fruits?

....

....

....

....

Did You Know?

In the land of Israel, the barley harvest takes place in March/April.

www.biblepathwayadventures.com
He is Risen! Activity Book

62

© BPA Publishing Ltd 202

Feast of First Fruits

Open your Bible to Matthew 28:5-6. Copy the scriptures on the lines provided.
Color the illustration at the bottom of the page.

www.biblepathwayadventures.com
...e is Risen! Activity Book

63

LESSON 5 | Lesson Plan
Galilee and the Ascension

Teacher: _____

Today's Bible passages: John 21:1-25, Acts 1:1-11

Welcome prayer:
Pray a simple prayer with the children before you begin the lesson.

Lesson objectives:
In this lesson, children will learn:
1. What happened when the disciples went fishing on the sea of Galilee
2. Yeshua's final instructions to His disciples

Did You Know?
Yeshua appeared to more than 500 people after He rose from the grave. (1 Corinthians 15:6)

Bible lesson overview:
The disciples traveled to Galilee. While they waited for Yeshua, they went fishing on the sea of Galilee. But they could hardly catch any fish. After a stranger told them to throw their nets overboard again, they quickly filled them with fish. Realizing the stranger was Yeshua, they quickly rowed their boat to shore and ate breakfast with Him. Yeshua gave His disciples an important job. "Go and make disciples of all nations. Teach them to do what I have shown you." Later on, before the Day of Pentecost (Shavu'ot), He met with them again in Jerusalem. Leading them to Bethany on the Mount of Olives, He ascended to heaven before their very eyes.

www.biblepathwayadventures.com
He is Risen! Activity Book

64

© BPA Publishing Ltd 202

Let's Review:

Questions to ask your students:

1. What instructions were the disciples given after they had caught no fish?
2. What question did Yeshua ask Peter? How many times?
3. What important instructions did Yeshua give His disciples?
4. Why did the disciples go back to Jerusalem?
5. Where did Yeshua ascend to heaven?

 ## A memory verse to help children remember God's Word:

"Go and make disciples…" (Matthew 28:19)

Activities:

Labyrinth: Help the disciples get to Galilee
Map activity: The Galilee
Worksheet: Israelite homes
Worksheet: Disciple facts
Let's learn Hebrew: Fish
Bible craft: Make a fish
Worksheet: What's the Word?
Question 'n color: Footsteps of the Messiah
Worksheet: Day of Pentecost
Coloring page: Go and make disciples
Worksheet: The Jerusalem Times
Bible quiz: The Ascension
Worksheet: The Holy Spirit
Worksheet: The Ascension
Worksheet: Acts 1:1-12

 ## Closing prayer:

End the lesson with a prayer.

ww.biblepathwayadventures.com
le is Risen! Activity Book

65

Help the disciples get to Galilee

Start

www.biblepathwayadventures.com
He is Risen! Activity Book

66

© BPA Publishing Ltd 202

The Galilee

Yeshua and His disciples spent a lot of time in Galilee, a region situated in northern Israel. The distance between Galilee and Jerusalem was estimated to be around 80 miles, taking up to a week to travel between the two places. Using the Internet or a historical atlas, mark the six Galilean towns and villages on the map: Iberias, Bethsaida, Gennesaret, Khersa, Magdala, and Capernaum. How did the disciples travel around Galilee?

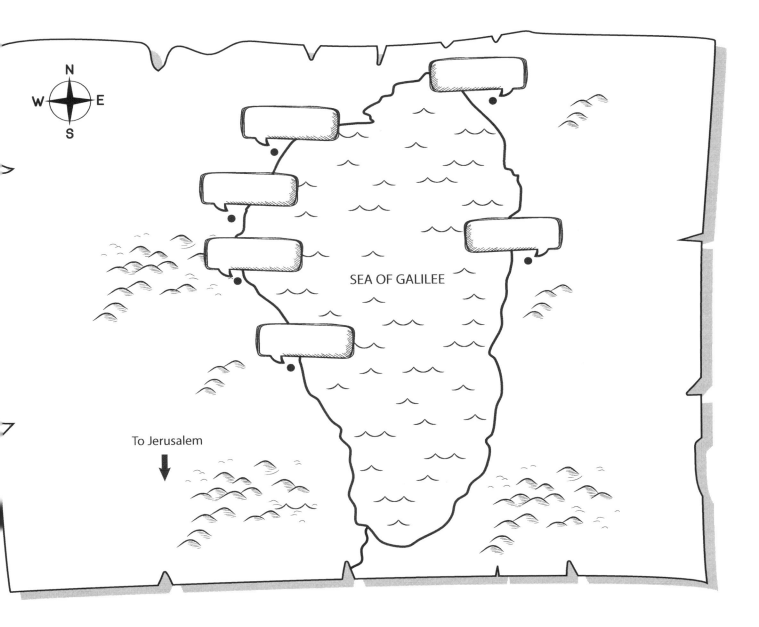

www.biblepathwayadventures.com
e is Risen! Activity Book

© BPA Publishing Ltd 2023

Israelite homes

During Bible times, many Israelite homes were small and plain.
They were built out of mud brick or stone, and roofs were made from branches or
straw covered in clay. During the night, domestic animals were kept in the stable area
to keep them safe from animals and robbers. What do you think? Did Peter and the
disciples live in this type of house in Capernaum? Color the picture.

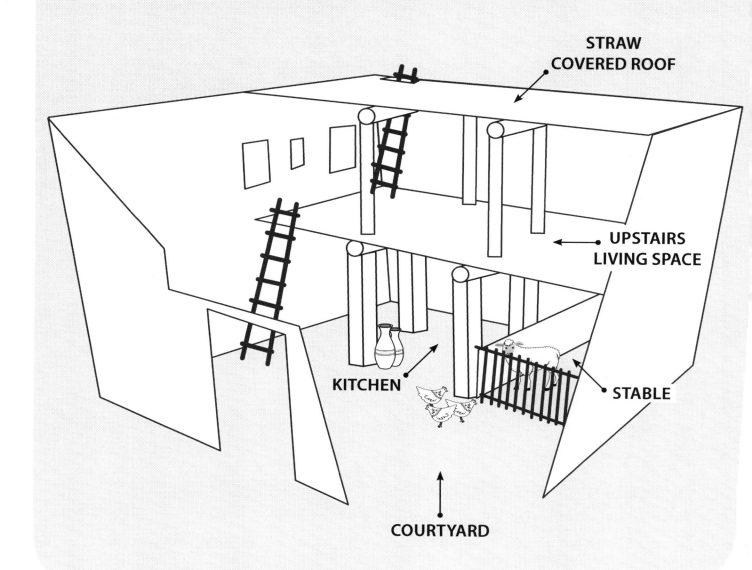

STRAW
COVERED ROOF

UPSTAIRS
LIVING SPACE

KITCHEN

STABLE

COURTYARD

www.biblepathwayadventures.com
He is Risen! Activity Book

68

© BPA Publishing Ltd 202

Disciple facts

Yeshua taught His disciples how to disciple others. Can you name some of Yeshua's closest disciples? Read the facts below and match them with the disciple.

1 A Judean, betrayed Yeshua for 30 pieces of silver, hung himself.

....

2 Greek name was Didymus, doubted the resurrection of Yeshua.

....

3 Brother of James, second name was Boanerges, which means son of Thunder, wrote the Gospel of John & Revelation.

....

4 Came from Bethsaida, one of the first disciples.

....

5 Son of Zebedee, preached in Jerusalem & Judea, was beheaded by Herod in AD 44.

....

6 Brother of Peter, fisherman, originally a disciple of John the Baptist.

....

7 Tax-collector, also called Levi.

....

8 Brother of James the Younger, he asked Yeshua at the Last Supper, "Why do you intend to show yourself to us and not to the world?" (John 14:22)

....

9 His name means Son of Tolmai, lived in Cana.

....

10 Fisherman, married, denied knowing Yeshua three times.

....

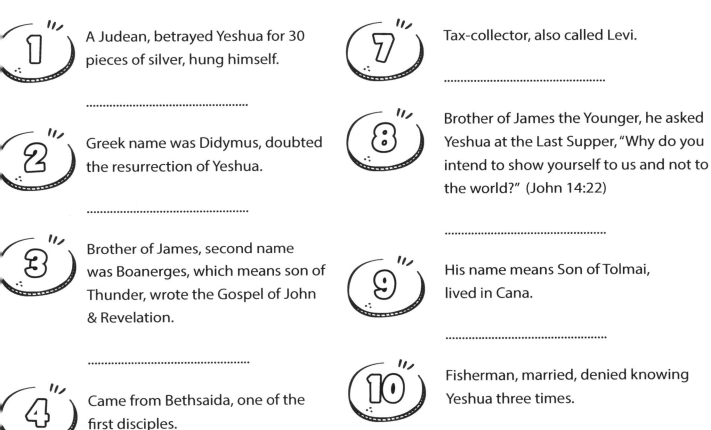

ANDREW	JUDAS
BARTHOLOMEW	JUDE (OR THADDEUS)
JAMES, SON OF ZEBEDEE	MATTHEW
THOMAS	PETER
JOHN	PHILIP

Dag

The Hebrew word for fish is dag. Some of the disciples (Andrew, Peter, James, and John) were fishermen. They lived in or near the village of Capernaum, and made a living catching fish on the Sea of Galilee.

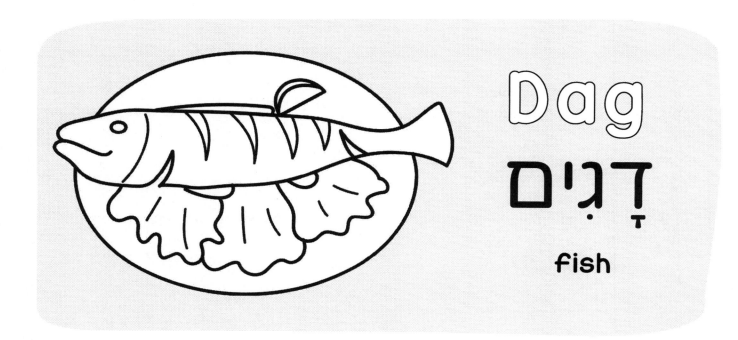

Dag

דָּגִים

fish

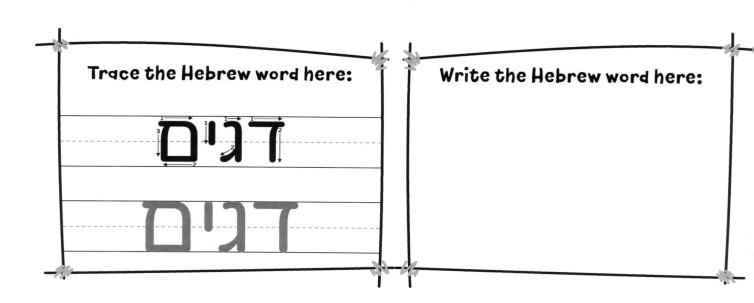

Trace the Hebrew word here:

דגים

דגים

Write the Hebrew word here:

www.biblepathwayadventures.com
He is Risen! Activity Book

70

© BPA Publishing Ltd 202

Let's write!

Practice writing this Hebrew word on the lines below.

דיוד

Try this on your own.
Remember that Hebrew is read from RIGHT to LEFT.

www.biblepathwayadventures.com
He is Risen! Activity Book

71

Make a Fish!

You will need:

1. Paper plates
2. Paint, felt pens, or crayons
3. Scissors and stapler (adults only)
4. Extra-strength glue sticks or school glue
5. Glitter, tissue paper, craft eyes, foil, sequins, etc

Instructions:

1. Cut out a triangle shape from the paper plate. Staple or glue it to the opposite side of the plate to create a tail.
2. Help your child to color their fish with paint or crayons.
3. Decorate your fish with craft eyes, glitter, tissue paper, sequins, etc.

ta-da!

www.biblepathwayadventures.com
He is Risen! Activity Book

72

What's the Word?

Read John 21:15-18 (ESV). Using the words below,
fill in the blanks to complete the Bible passage.

BREAKFAST	LOVE	WALK	YESHUA
LAMBS	DRESS	CARRY	THIRD

" When they had finished ...., Yeshua said to Simon Peter, "Simon, son of John, do you love Me more than these?" He said to Him, "Yes, Master; you know that I love you." He said to him, "Feed My ...." Yeshua said to him a second time, "Simon, son of John, do you love Me?" He said to him, "Yes, Master; you know that I love you." He said to him, "Tend My sheep." He said to him the third time, "Simon, son of John, do you .... Me?" 'Peter was grieved because Yeshua said to him the .... time, "Do you love me?" and he said to Him, "Master, you know everything; you know that I love you." .... said to him, "Feed my sheep. Truly, truly, I say to you, when you were young you used to .... yourself and .... wherever you wanted. But when you are old, you will stretch out your hands and another will dress you and .... you where you do not want to go." "

www.biblepathwayadventures.com
He is Risen! Activity Book

73

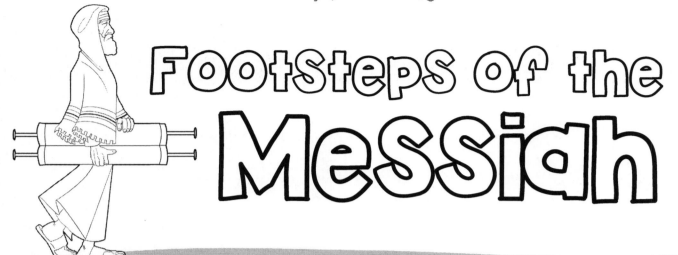

Footsteps of the Messiah

The only Bible available at the time of Yeshua was the Old Testament. When He spoke to the Israelites, He often quoted from the Old Testament (Tanakh). Read and answer the questions below.

1. Which Old Testament verse did Yeshua quote in Matthew 27:46 and Mark 15:34?

   ....

   ....

2. Which Old Testament verses did Yeshua quote in Matthew 13:14-15?

   ....

   ....

3. Which Old Testament verse did Yeshua quote in Luke 19:46?

   ....

   ....

www.biblepathwayadventures.com
He is Risen! Activity Book

74

Day of Pentecost

Fifty days after the Feast of First Fruits (the day Yeshua rose from the grave) is the Day of Pentecost (Shavu'ot). Pentecost is one of God's Feasts and is also known as the feast of 'Weeks'. During biblical times, it was one of three Appointed Times that Israelite men were expected to travel to Jerusalem to honor. When Yeshua ascended to heaven, the discipleswere in Jerusalem waiting to celebrate this Feast.

According to some Bible historians, Shavu'ot also marks the time the twelve tribes of Israel were given the Ten Commandments on Mount Sinai. Peter and the disciples were in Jerusalem for Shavu'ot when tongues like fire descended, and many pilgrims understood what the disciples were saying in their own language. Some Bible scholars believe these pilgrims were descendants of the ten tribes of Israel scattered among the nations.

1. Why were Peter and the disciples in Jerusalem at this time?

....

2. Name two events in the Bible that happened on Shavu'ot.

....

....

Color the Israelite!

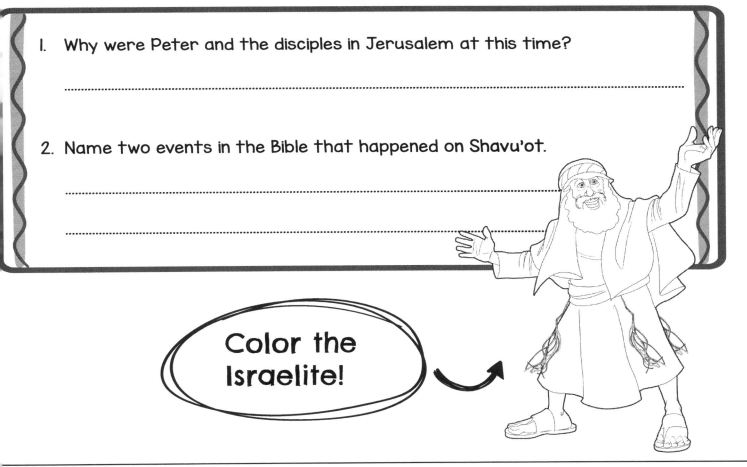

ww.biblepathwayadventures.com
e is Risen! Activity Book

75

Go and make disciples

Yeshua told His disciples to make disciples of all nations (Matthew 28:19). After His death, where did the disciples go? Read Matthew 10 and discuss where they may have traveled. Color the picture.

Who are the lost sheep of the House of Israel?

www.biblepathwayadventures.com
He is Risen! Activity Book

76

City of Jerusalem

The
Jerusalem Times

| ACTS 2 | DAY OF PENTECOST | A BIBLE HISTORY PUBLICATION |

Day of worship

....

....

....

....

....

....

Israelites celebrate Shavu'ot

....

....

....

Pilgrims arrive!

www.biblepathwayadventures.com
e is Risen! Activity Book

77

© BPA Publishing Ltd 2023

The ASCENSION

Read Matthew 28:16-20, Mark 16:19-20, John 21 and Acts 1:1-12. Answer the questions below.

(1) After Yeshua rose from the grave, how long did He stay on earth before He rose to Heaven?

(2) After Yeshua appeared to His disciples in Jerusalem, where did they next meet Him?

(3) Who dove into the water and swam towards Yeshua?

(4) What did Yeshua ask Peter three times?

(5) What did Yeshua promise His disciples before He rose to Heaven?

(6) Where did Yeshua say His disciples would go and tell people about Him?

(7) On which mount did Yeshua ascend to Heaven?

(8) As Yeshua ascended, what hid Him from the eyes of those watching?

(9) Who appeared to the disciples after Yeshua rose to Heaven?

(10) What did these men tell the disciples?

www.biblepathwayadventures.com
He is Risen! Activity Book

78

© BPA Publishing Ltd 202

The Holy Spirit

Read John 16:8. The role of
the Holy Spirit is to....

....

....

....

....

....

....

....

....

Read I John 3:4. The Bible says
that sin is…

....

....

....

....

....

....

....

The fruit of the Holy Spirit
in my life is…

....

....

....

....

....

....

Read Deuteronomy 6:24-25.
We are righteous if we…

....

....

....

....

....

....

The Ascension

"When they had come together, the disciples asked Him, "Master, will you at this time restore the kingdom to Israel?" He said to them, "It is not for you to know times or seasons that the Father has fixed by His own authority. But you will receive power when the Holy Spirit has come upon you, and you will be My witnesses in Jerusalem and in all Judea and Samaria, and to the end of the earth." When He had said these things, as they were looking on, He was lifted up, and a cloud took Him out of their sight. And while they were gazing into heaven as He went, two men stood by them in white robes, and said, "Men of Galilee, why do you stand looking into heaven? This Yeshua, who was taken up from you into heaven, will come in the same way as you saw Him go into heaven." Then they returned to Jerusalem from the mount called Olivet, which is near Jerusalem, a Sabbath day's journey away." (Acts 1:6-12)

Read Acts 1:1-12. Answer the questions below.

1. What did the disciples ask Yeshua when they had come together?

2. What did Yeshua tell the disciples?

3. What happened when Yeshua said these things?

4. What did the two men in white robes tell the disciples?

www.biblepathwayadventures.com
He is Risen! Activity Book

80

Acts 1:1-12

Write a short summary

....

....

....

....

Today God showed me...

....

....

....

| Key Verse | Key People | Key Idea |

www.biblepathwayadventures.com
...e is Risen! Activity Book

81

Crafts &
Projects

www.biblepathwayadventures.com
He is Risen! Activity Book

82

© BPA Publishing Ltd 202

Make a
Paper Plate Golgotha

You will need:

1. Paper plate (one per child)
2. Paint, felt pens, or crayons
3. School glue, glue stick, or a stapler
4. Scissors (adults only)

Instructions:

1. Cut a paper plate in half. Color the plate green (for grass).
2. Cut out the printable crosses on the next page. Color the crosses brown (for wood).
3. Glue or staple the three crosses onto the top of the paper plate.

1.   **2.**   **3.**

ta-da!

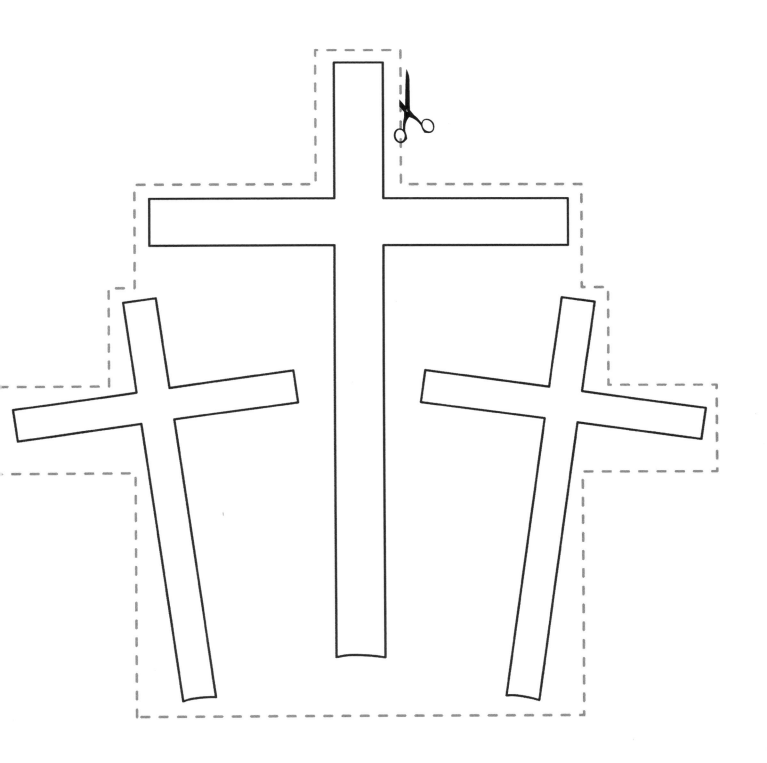

e is Risen! Activity Book

Make a
Paper Plate Tomb

You will need:

1. Two thick foam or paper plates (use the sturdy kind with a "lip")
2. Heavy card stock
3. Grey paint or crayons
4. Yeshua and the angel Bible characters (see next page)
5. Scissors (adult only)
6. Extra-strength glue sticks or School glue

Preparation:

Print the Yeshua and angel Bible characters. Make copies onto heavy card stock and cut out the characters.

Instructions:

1. Cut the bottoms off both paper plates so they can stand up.
2. Paint or color the paper plates grey. Remember to color the front and back!
3. While the paper plate is drying, ask the children to color Yeshua and the angel.
4. Cut out a door on one paper plate. Glue both paper plates together to form a tomb.
5. Glue your cardboard Yeshua and angel onto the tomb.

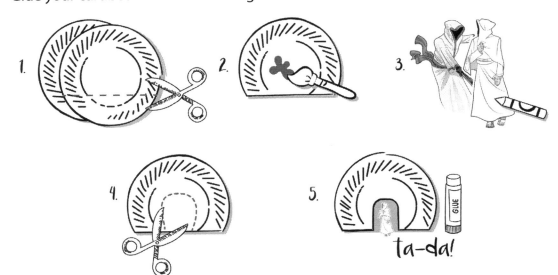

Bible characters: Yeshua and the angel.

Bible story cards

He is Risen!

ww.biblepathwayadventures.com
e is Risen! Activity Book

91

Triumphal Entry

The disciples went and did as Yeshua asked. They brought the donkey and the colt and put on them their cloaks, and He sat on them. Most of the crowd spread their cloaks on the road, and others cut branches from the trees and spread them on the road. The crowds that went before Him and that followed Him were shouting, "Hosanna to the Son of David! Blessed is He who comes in the name of God! Hosanna in the highest!"

Matthew 21:6-9

 Matthew 21:1-11

The Last Supper

As they were eating, Yeshua took bread, and after blessing it broke it and gave it to the disciples, and said, "Take, eat; this is My body." And He took a cup, and when He had given thanks He gave it to them, saying, "Drink of it, all of you, for this is My blood of the covenant, which is poured out for many for the forgiveness of sins. I tell you I will not drink again of this fruit of the vine until that day when I drink it new with you in My Father's kingdom."

Matthew 26:26-29

 Matthew 26:17-30

Betrayal

Then one of the twelve, whose name was Judas Iscariot, went to the chief priests and said, "What will you give me if I deliver Him over to you?" And they paid him thirty pieces of silver. And from that moment Judas sought an opportunity to betray Him.

Matthew 26:14-16

 Matthew 26:14-46

Garden of Gethsemane

While Yeshua was still speaking, Judas came, one of the twelve, and with him a great crowd with swords and clubs, from the chief priests and the elders of the people. Now the betrayer had given them a sign, saying, "The one I will kiss is the man; seize him." And he came up to Jesus at once and said, "Greetings, Rabbi!" And he kissed him. Yeshua said to him, "Friend, do what you came to do." Then they came up and laid hands on Yeshua and seized him.

Matthew 26:47-50

Matthew 26:36-56

Yeshua Before Caiaphas

Those who had seized Yeshua led Him to Caiaphas the high priest, where the scribes and the elders had gathered. And Peter was following him at a distance, as far as the courtyard of the high priest, and going inside he sat with the guards to see the end. Now the chief priests and the whole council were seeking false testimony against Yeshua that they might put Him to death, but they found none, though many false witnesses came forward.

Matthew 26:57-60

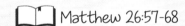 Matthew 26:57-68

Peter's Denial

A servant girl came up to Peter and said, "You were with Yeshua the Galilean." But he denied it, saying, "I do not know what you mean." When he went out to the entrance, another girl saw him, and said to the bystanders, "This man was with Yeshua of Nazareth." Again, he said, "I do not know the man." After a while the bystanders came to Peter and said, "You are one of them. Your accent betrays you." Peter began to invoke a curse on himself and to swear, "I do not know the man." Immediately the rooster crowed. Peter remembered the saying of Yeshua, "Before the temple crier blows the shofar, you will deny me three times."

Matthew 26:69-75

Matthew 26:30-75

Yeshua Before Pilate

Yeshua stood before Pilate, and the governor asked Him, "Are you the King of the Jews?" Yeshua said, "You have said so." But when he was accused by the chief priests and elders, he gave no answer. Then Pilate said to Him, "Do you not hear how many things they testify against you?" But He gave him no answer, not even to a single charge, so that Pilate was greatly amazed.

Matthew 27:11-14

 Matthew 27:11-26

The Crucifixion

They crucified two rebels with Him, one on His right and one on His left. Those who passed by hurled insults at Him, shaking their heads and saying, "So! You who are going to destroy the temple and build it in three days, come down from the cross and save yourself!" In the same way the chief priests and the Torah teachers mocked Him. "He saved others but He can't save himself! Let this Messiah, this king of Israel, come down now from the cross, that we may see and believe." Those crucified with Him also heaped insults on Him.

Mark 15:27-32

Mark 15:21-40

ww.biblepathwayadventures.com
e is Risen! Activity Book

95

The Passover

They shall take some of the blood and put it on the two doorposts and the lintel of the houses in which they eat it. They shall eat the flesh that night, roasted on the fire; with unleavened bread and bitter herbs they shall eat it.

Exodus 12:7-8

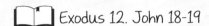 Exodus 12. John 18-19

He is Risen!

The angel said to the women, "Do not be afraid, for I know that you are looking for Yeshua, who was crucified. He is not here; He has risen, just as He said. Come and see the place where He lay Then go quickly and tell His disciples: 'He has risen from the dead and is going ahead of you into Galilee. There you will see him.' Now I have told you."

Matthew 28:5-7

Matthew 28:1-20

The Great Commission

The eleven disciples went to Galilee, to the mountain where Yeshua had told them to go. When they saw Him, they worshiped Him; but some doubted. Yeshua came to them and said, "All authority in heaven and on earth has been given to Me. Go and make disciples of all nations, baptizing them in the name of the Father, the Son and the Holy Spirit. Teach them to obey everything I have commanded you. I am with you always, to the end of the age."

Matthew 28:16-20

Matthew 28:1-20

The Ascension

When Yeshua had said these things, as they were looking on, He was lifted up, and a cloud took Him out of their sight. And while they were gazing into heaven as He went, two men stood by them in white robes, and said, "Men of Galilee, why do you stand looking into heaven? This Yeshua, who was taken up from you into heaven, will come in the same way as you saw Him go into heaven."

Acts 1:9-11

Acts 1:1-12

ANSWER KEY

Lesson One: The last supper

Let's Review:

To eat a meal together

Judas told the religious leaders where they could find Yeshua

Yeshua washed His disciples' feet

To a garden on the Mount of Olives (called Gethsemane)

The disciples deserted Yeshua and ran away

Bible quiz: The last supper

In a furnished upper room in Jerusalem

Bread and wine

Yeshua washed His disciples' feet

Judas

"Love one another just as I have loved you. By this, all people will know that you are My disciples."

Simon Peter

Who will be regarded as the greatest

Keep His commandments

The Holy Spirit (Helper)

). To a garden on the Mount of Olives

Bible word search: The last supper

```
Z B C T Q D Y Z G D O B U C K
L H C I F E O E A W N O X U O
Q J Y A E A R H S I T D S P R
J U D A S W T A A H M Y Z O C
J K O W S I S H S W U T Z R O
B L O O D L M R E E N A Y J M
K H F Y S V R S M R O M Q T M
S E M N M Y L S K I K J E G A
Z C O V E N A N T A N N U K N
M W S Q P G W K N X A F W W D
E B D G D Q D H N J L P V P M
U P P E R R O O M Y V O Z I E
B R E A D F M F G W F Y E N N
V G M M D I S C I P L E S P T
C G L W A S H F E E T S G K D
```

Worksheet: Unleavened Bread

Question 2 answer:

[Se]ven days you shall eat unleavened bread. On the first day you [sh]all remove leaven out of your houses, for if anyone eats what [is] leavened, from the first day until the seventh day, that person [sh]all be cut off from Israel. On the first day you shall hold a holy [a]ssembly, and on the seventh day a holy assembly. No work [sh]all be done on those days. But what everyone needs to eat, [th]at alone may be prepared by you. And you shall observe [t]he Feast of Unleavened Bread, for on this very day I brought your hosts out of the land of Egypt. Therefore, you shall observe this day, throughout your generations, as a statute forever. In the first month, from the fourteenth day of the month at evening, you shall eat unleavened bread until the twenty-first day of the month at evening. For seven days no leaven is to be found in your houses.

Worksheet: What's the Word?

When it was evening, He reclined at table with the twelve. As they were eating, He said, "Truly I say to you, one of you will betray Me." They were very sorrowful and began to say to Him one after another, "Is it I, Master?" He answered, "He who has dipped his hand in the dish with Me will betray Me. The Son of Man goes as it is written of Him, but woe to that man by whom the Son of Man is betrayed! It would have been better for that man if he had not been born." Judas, who would betray Him, answered, "Is it I, Rabbi?" He said to him, "You have said so." Now as they were eating, Yeshua took bread, and after blessing it broke it and gave it to the disciples, and said, "Take, eat; this is My body." And He took a cup, and when He had given thanks He gave it to them, saying, "Drink of it, all of you, for this is My blood of the covenant, which is poured out for many for the forgiveness of sins. I tell you I will not drink again of this fruit of the vine until that day when I drink it new with you in My Father's kingdom."

Bible quiz: Mount of Olives

1. In Jerusalem
2. Gethsemane
3. The three disciples fell asleep
4. Simon Peter
5. With a kiss
6. An angel
7. 30 pieces of silver
8. The Feast of Unleavened Bread
9. The deserted Yeshua and ran away
10. They first took Yeshua to Annas, the father-in-law of Caiaphas, the High Priest. Then they took Yeshua to see Caiaphas and the Sanhedrin

Worksheet: The religious leaders

1. The religious leaders made rules about the religious life of the Hebrew people, and they were also rulers and judges
2. Many religious leaders (like the chief priests and high priest) lived in luxury. They funded their lavish lifestyles with a temple tax that the Hebrew people had to pay. These temple taxes combined with taxes imposed by Herod and Rome were a huge burden that kept many people in poverty

Lesson Two: Road to Golgotha
Let's Review:
1. The ancient Jewish court system was called the Sanhedrin, made up of 70 religious leaders and the high priest
2. Only Pontius Pilate (the Roman governor) could sentence someone to die
3. Judas returned the money because he was filled with remorse
4. Yeshua was nailed to the stake at a place called Golgotha
5. Two criminals were crucified beside Yeshua at Golgotha

Bible quiz: Pontius Pilate
1. Roman governor
2. Jerusalem
3. Judgment seat
4. Barabbas
5. "Have nothing to do with that just Man, for I have suffered many things in a dream because of Him."
6. Crucify Him
7. "I am innocent of the blood of this just Person. You see to it."
8. Crown of thorns
9. Joseph of Arimathea
10. The religious leaders were worried that Yeshua's disciples would steal His body

Worksheet: Who was Pontius Pilate?
1. Pilate was accused of harsh behavior, pride, violence, greed, holding executions without trial, and horrible cruelty towards the Hebrew people
2. A limestone block with an inscription that says, "Pontius Pilate, Prefect of Judea."

Comprehension worksheet: The Temple Crier
Answer to question #1:
Chickens were banned as they flew into and defiled the temple

Question 'n color: Journey to Golgotha
1. Pilate, the Roman governor
2. A crossbeam
3. Yeshua of Nazareth, King of the Jews

Bible quiz: Betrayal
1. Disciples
2. A piece of bread
3. The religious leaders (chief priests)
4. 30 pieces of silver
5. Garden of Gethsemane
6. With a kiss
7. Master
8. Aceldama (Potter's Field)
9. Joseph and Matthias
10. Matthias

Lesson Three: The crucifixion
Let's Review:
1. "You were going to destroy the Temple and rebuild it in three days. Come down from the cross if you are the Son of God. If you are the Messiah, save yourself and us."
2. Lambs were slaughtered for the Passover meal later that evening
3. "My Father, into Your hands I place My spirit."
4. An earthquake rocked the city, rocks split open, and a veil the temple ripped from top to bottom
5. A Roman soldier pierced Yeshua's side with a spear

Bible quiz: Death on the stake
1. Pilate, the Roman Governor
2. Simon of Cyrene
3. Golgotha
4. King of the Judeans
5. My God, my God, why have you forsaken me?
6. Two criminals
7. Three hours
8. Joseph of Arimathea
9. Spear
10. Linen cloth

Coloring worksheet: Crucifixion
1. The curtain (veil) at the temple
2. An earthquake
3. The centurion and guards who were guarding Yeshua

Bible quiz: The Passover meal
1. God sent ten plagues on Egypt
2. Painted lamb's blood on the door-posts and lintel of their homes
3. Tenth day of the first month (Aviv)
4. At twilight on the 14th day of the first month (Aviv)
5. Lamb, bread, and bitter herbs
6. Unleavened bread (Matzah)
7. The Feast of Unleavened Bread
8. Throughout their generations (forever)
9. Golgotha
10. Yeshua was of the tribe of Judah, one of the 12 tribes of Israel

Bible word scramble: Who pierced the Messiah's body?
"But one of the soldiers pierced his side with a spear, and at once there came out blood and water." (John 19:34)

www.biblepathwayadventures.com
He is Risen! Activity Book

100

© BPA Publishing Ltd 20

le crossword: The cross and empty tomb

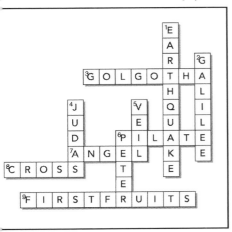

orksheet: The temple
One reason Herod enlarged the Temple Mount was to accommodate the large number of pilgrims who came to Jerusalem for the Feast of Unleavened Bread, Pentecost (Shavu'ot), and Tabernacles (Sukkot)

Israelites who wished to sacrifice formed groups. Each group slaughtered one Passover lamb for that bunch of people. The Passover lamb, unlike the usual animal offerings, was sacrificed by the Israelites themselves. As with all peace offerings, it was offered in the inner court and its blood tossed on the altar. After one group completed the ritual, the doors were opened again and the next group entered. The lambs were roasted and eaten that night

orksheet: True or false?
e soldiers divided Yeshua's garments into six parts (false)
e soldiers broke Yeshua's legs (false)
ood and water poured out of Yeshua's body (true)
ter Yeshua died, many holy people who had died were raised
life (true)
here was a notice above Yeshua's head, which read: This is the
ng of the Jews (true)
eshua saw His grandfather standing near the cross (false)

esson Four: He is Risen!
et's Review:
Joseph of Arimathea
The priests were afraid that Yeshua's disciples would come and steal His body away
An angel

4. "Do not be afraid, for I know that you seek Yeshua who was crucified. He is not here, for he has risen, as he said. Come, see the place where he lay."
5. The priests paid the guards a bribe not to tell anyone what they had seen

Bible quiz: The resurrection
1. An angel
2. First Fruits, during the week of Unleavened Bread
3. Money
4. Mary Magdalene
5. An empty tomb
6. "Why do you seek the living among the dead? 6 He is not here, but has risen."
7. Thomas
8. Sea of Galilee
9. 40 days (Acts 1:3)
10. Go and make disciples

Bible word search: He is risen!

Worksheet: The chief priests
1. A group of Roman soldiers
2. A bribe (money)
3. His disciples came by night and stole him away while we were asleep

Worksheet: What's the Word?
After the Sabbath toward the dawn of the first day of the week, Mary Magdalene and the other Mary went to see the tomb. And behold, there was a great earthquake, for an angel of God descended from heaven and rolled back the stone and sat on it. His appearance was like lightning, and his clothing white as

ww.biblepathwayadventures.com
e is Risen! Activity Book

101

snow. And for fear of him the guards trembled and became like dead men. But the angel said to the women, "Do not be afraid, for I know that you seek Yeshua who was crucified. He is not here, for He has risen, as he said. Come, see the place where He lay. Then go quickly and tell His disciples that He has risen from the dead. He is going before you to Galilee; there you will see Him.

Bible quiz: Mary Magdalene
1. Seven demons
2. Yeshua's mother and her sister, and Mary wife of Clopas
3. Joseph of Arimathea
4. The Sabbath
5. Who will roll away the stone from the entrance of the tomb?
6. An Angel
7. Mary Magdalene
8. The gardener
9. He had not yet ascended to the Father
10. I have seen Yeshua!

Coloring worksheet: Mary Magdalene
1. An angel
2. Mary Magdalene
3. "I have seen Yeshua!"

Lesson Five: Galilee and the Ascension
Let's Review:
1. Throw their net overboard again
2. Peter, do you love me? Three times
3. Go and make disciples
4. To gather for the Day of Pentecost (Feast of Shavu'ot)
5. Bethany, a village on the Mount of Olives

Worksheet: Disciple facts
Andrew = 6, Bartholomew = 9, James, son of Zebedee = 5, Judas = 1, John = 3, Jude = 8, Matthew = 7, Peter = 10, Philip = 4, Thomas = 2

Worksheet: What's the Word?
When they had finished breakfast, Yeshua said to Simon Peter, "Simon, son of John, do you love Me more than these?" He said to Him, "Yes, Master; you know that I love you." He said to him, "Feed My lambs." Yeshua said to him a second time, "Simon, son of John, do you love Me?" He said to him, "Yes, Master; you know that I love you." He said to him, "Tend My sheep." He said to him the third time, "Simon, son of John, do you love Me?" Peter was grieved because he said to Him the third time, "Do you love me?" and he said to him, "Master, you

know everything; you know that I love you." Yeshua said to him, "Feed my sheep. Truly, truly, I say to you, when you were young you used to dress yourself and walk wherever you wanted. But when you are old, you will stretch out your hands and another will dress you and carry you where you do not want to go."

Worksheet: Footsteps of the Messiah
1. Psalm 22:2
2. Isaiah 6:9-10
3. Jeremiah 7:11

Worksheet: Day of Pentecost
1. To honor the Day of Pentecost (Shavu'ot)
2. The giving of the Ten Commandments at Mount Sinai, and tongues of fire

Bible quiz: The Ascension
1. Forty days
2. Sea of Galilee
3. Peter
4. Do you love Me?
5. The Holy Spirit (Ruach HaKodesh)
6. Judea, Samaria and to many other countries
7. Mount of Olives
8. A cloud
9. Two men dressed in white
10. Yeshua will return to you the same way He left

Worksheet: The Ascension
1. The disciples asked Yeshua if He would at that time restore the kingdom to Israel
2. Yeshua told the disciples that it was not for them to know times or seasons that the Father has fixed by His own authority. He also told them that they would receive power when the Holy Spirit had come upon them, and they would be His witnesses in Jerusalem and in all Judea and Samaria and to the end of the earth
3. When Yeshua said these things, He was lifted up and a cloud took Him out of their sight
4. The two men in white robes told the disciples that Yeshua, who was taken up from them into heaven, would come in the same way as they saw Him go into heaven

www.biblepathwayadventures.com
He is Risen! Activity Book

102

◇ DISCOVER MORE ACTIVITY BOOKS! ◇

Available for purchase at www.biblepathwayadventures.com

INSTANT DOWNLOAD!

100 Bible Quizzes   Bereshit / Genesis

100 Bible Word Search   Moses Ten Plagues

He is Risen!   Birth of The King

He is Risen! (Beginners)   Bible Miracles

Made in the USA
Las Vegas, NV
28 June 2023